THE SPIRIT OF
ENTERPRISE

Matt Bird Publishing

PO Box 38082

London

SW19 1YW

UK

www.mattbirdpublishing.com

Thanks to

David Blakelock, Jane Gould-Smith
and Nurden Cross.

Contents

Foreword

Matt is about to tell you this in his introduction, but the purpose of this book is to "catalyze an outbreak of the spirit of enterprise." Now, in the introduction, Matt is going to spell catalyze with an s, which should signal to you that he and I are from opposite sides of "the pond," if you will. But while we live in entirely different parts of the globe, I can't help but feel incredibly connected to the work he is doing.

When The Times newspaper published the article, "It's time for faith-driven entrepreneurs to emerge," I couldn't get permission to share it on the Faith Driven Entrepreneur website fast enough. While there was an obvious branding decision to be made, we really wanted to share it because what Matt wrote gets at the heartbeat of what we at Faith Driven Entrepreneur and Faith Driven Investor want to see happen all around the globe.

There is a growing movement of faithful followers of Christ who have realized that God has given them something. That something may be an inkling of an idea, a newly founded business, a late-stage startup, or capital to invest in one, if not all, of those three. Regardless, Christians are starting to realize that these things—these roles and responsibilities, these opportunities and options—were given to them by God. And when we understand that God is the owner of our businesses and our finances and that we are the stewards, everything begins to change.

Suddenly, we come alive with a new purpose. We're no longer working for a bigger payday, a better IPO, a greater return to fund that second house. We realize that our core identity is as beloved children of God and that as we focus on "being" rather than "doing," interestingly we then have an incredible opportunity to do great work not for ourselves but for God—and along the way, we feel his pleasure.

The Spirit of Enterprise is proof that now is the time. The world is waiting for faithful people to step into their God-given purpose and pursue their call to create. The world needs men and women whose lives have been transformed by the Gospel, who have accepted the gift of salvation, and who live, work, and breathe out of their unshakeable identities in Christ. If you're reading this, I hope you're one of those people. I also hope that you know you're not alone.

There are approximately 538 million entrepreneurs in the world. That's 538 million men and women who are creating and shaping culture. 538 million men and women who already know the argument Matt makes in his article, and now in this book. Entrepreneurs know that their work is an opportunity to transform and innovate, to help and serve, to launch and learn.

But where the faith driven entrepreneur has a distinct advantage is that they're doing all of that not for themselves, but for the God they know, love, and serve. There's nothing better than that. And frankly, there's no better time for it either.

The world needs you. God wants to use you. Stop waiting, and step into your chance to make an impact in the unique time you've found yourself in.

You're not the only one who's here. Come join the other faith inspired entrepreneurs and find out what happens when your purpose unites with God's plan to serve all people all around the world.

Henry Kaestner
Founder of Faith Driven Entrepreneur

We need an outbreak of something more powerful than a virus: the spirit of enterprise.

Introduction

This book was inspired by the response I received to an article that I wrote for The Times newspaper, which was published on 23 January 2021:

'It's time for faith-driven entrepreneurs to emerge' :

As the pandemic continues, we need an outbreak of something more powerful than a virus: the spirit of enterprise. It is time for new business enterprises that create value and jobs, to replace the hundreds of thousands being lost. We need initiatives that can create social glue, capable of bringing the disparate parts of our lonely and isolated society together.

As a follower of Jesus, my go-to place for inspiration is the Bible, which says, "Remember the Lord your God, for it is he who gives you the ability to produce wealth." (Deuteronomy 8:18). Clearly, wealth creation is a gift of God, not a gift of capitalism.

The word 'wealth', which has come to mean financial abundance, derives from the old English word 'weal', meaning wellness and wellbeing. True wealth is not simply the sum of our cash and assets, but is also the relational capital that exists in our families, communities and society. This is the essence of the Hebrew word Shalom, which means peace, harmony, completeness, welfare and prosperity.

God's gift of wealth , creation can unleash untold levels of human flourishing and thriving.

The "Faith Driven Entrepreneur" movement explains, "We believe that business has God-given power to transform nations by creating jobs, generating prosperity and catalysing human flourishing" - an entrepreneurship, not driven by motives of selfish ambition and greed, but rather of compassion and a desire to benefit all.

Cinnamon Network International, the charity of which I am founder, has been busier than ever during the pandemic, supporting social entrepreneurs to scale community impact. Our partners in the UK are opening community 'listening ear' centres; in South Africa, thousands of face masks are being produced to protect key workers; and in Australia, they are training volunteers to reduce the tragic growth of domestic violence. Cinnamon is supporting these social entrepreneurs to replicate their approaches to save others having to reinvent the wheel.

In the UK the number of companies formed in the second half of 2020 soared compared to the same time the previous year. According to the Office for National Statistics, there are more than 13,000 companies being formed every week compared to 11,000 during the same time the previous year.

Whilst high street spending is down, we are seeing the "at home" market grow. At home medical testing, sports equipment, education platforms, family entertainment, and food and wine experiences are growing rapidly. These market changes are not temporal, so initiating a new enterprise NOW will build benefits for years to come.

As the old saying goes, "necessity is the mother of invention". Let's innovate, launch and grow rather than pause, retreat and retrench.

Maybe you have a creative, enterprising or innovative idea, an idea that could be deployed to create wealth and wellbeing in your community, across our country and around the world?

From my experience in coaching entrepreneurs, the greatest barriers are self-limiting beliefs. We might think that our idea, resources or experience are too small to come to much. God is in the habit of taking the little we offer him — such as the boy who offered Jesus five small loaves and two fish to help feed a crowd — and making a lot out of it. On that occasion the crowd of 5,000 people were fed and there was more to spare.

At other times the resistance to our idea may come from those we try and get on board in the early stages. It may be an angel investor, strategic partner or board member. Recently, a friend reached out to someone with a powerful idea. They were pushed away with the response that they weren't taking on anything new until after the pandemic. I can't help but think that it could be a slightly longer wait than they think.

It's actually the spirit of innovation, creativity and enterprise that will help pull us through this pandemic. Let's overcome our feelings of self-doubt and fear of rejection and failure and instead dig deep in our reservoirs of determination, hope and compassion.

Now is the perfect time to launch a new venture.

There is no shortage of human need and opportunity or the people talent, technology and financial capital required. Let us unleash the spirit of enterprise to create livelihoods and well-being: true wealth and shalom.

On reading the article an Australian friend, who is a partner in a leading law firm, was inspired to write the following prayer.

Praying this would make the perfect start to this book...

As I kneel

And to my Maker appeal

For Him to reveal

The real deal

For us to seal

I also feel

That I should heal

Praying not simply for a meal

But love and zeal

And especially for weal

Amen

My hope is that this book is not simply something you will read, but something you will use to catalyse an outbreak of the spirit of enterprise.

Please would you gather people who want to discover an idea that could turn into a money making business, who have an idea that they have always wanted to get off the ground or create employment opportunities for others as well as for themselves.

If you gather a handful then start off a Spirit of Enterprise Group, or if a dozen or more then start a Spirit of Enterprise Network.

Use this book as a workbook to guide people through the 7 steps to starting a business that creates human flourishing for others.

Matt Bird
www.thespiritofenterprise.net

Your 'why' is your manifesto and motivation. It sets out the reason for the existence of your enterprise. It is only when your 'why' is in place that you can start to plan how to achieve it.

Session 1

Transformation not Transaction

Introduction

According to Andrew Wilkinson, the founder of international tech firm MetaLab, not all entrepreneurs are driven by money. He says, "The siren call for many entrepreneurs isn't money, it's freedom. The freedom to chart your own path, the freedom to build what you want with the people you love."

The comment demonstrates that Wilkinson's 'why' is at the heart of what he does: he wants freedom and not the restrictions of a corporate structure developed by someone else.

If you don't know your 'why' at the start of your enterprise, you will fail to figure out the 'how'. As a result, you are more likely to struggle when life throws curveballs that could unsettle you. Worse still, when plans are no longer running at full speed or how you want them, you will lose traction and become lethargic.

Your 'why' is your manifesto and motivation. It sets out the reason for the existence of your enterprise. It is only when your 'why' is in place that you can start to plan how to achieve it.

German philosopher Frederick Nietzsche once said, "He who has a why can endure any how."

Enduring is not something to enjoy, but there are times in life when difficulties happen and endurance is the key to success. At these times refocusing on your 'why' will motivate you during moments of inertia.

What motivates you?

One of the courses I run through my business Relationology is 'Writing My Book', which helps people become first-time published authors. In the first session, we talk about the 'why' behind writing a book.

Delegates use a 'motivation spider', which is an 8-point infographic that, when completed, resembles a spider's web. The points that make up this graph represent different motivations include 'income generation', 'brand building' and 'increasing influence'.

The 'motivation spider' helps chart the genuine reasons of the 'why' behind each person's purpose. Having this information to hand helps when you can't see the wood from the trees, which will inevitably happen when setting up an enterprise.

It's not that you will lose focus or interest when starting an enterprise, but dealing with necessary paperwork or legal requirements can be demotivating. In those times, you can feel lost, so use your 'why' as your 'true north'. Pick up your compass, set it to 'true north' and rediscover that 'why'! It will always be your motivation.

Reading: Jesus declares his 'why'

In **Luke 4: 14-21** Jesus declares his 'why' confidently for his life and work.

14 Jesus returned to Galilee in the power of the Spirit, and news about him spread through the whole countryside. 15 He was teaching in their synagogues, and everyone praised him. 16 He went to Nazareth, where he had been brought up, and on the Sabbath day he went into the synagogue, as was his custom. He stood up to read, 17 and the scroll of the prophet Isaiah was handed to him. Unrolling it, he found the place where it is written:

18 "The Spirit of the Lord is on me,
  because he has anointed me
  to proclaim good news to the poor.
He has sent me to proclaim freedom for the prisoners
  and recovery of sight for the blind,
to set the oppressed free,
19   to proclaim the year of the Lord's favour."

20 Then he rolled up the scroll, gave it back to the attendant and sat down. The eyes of everyone in the synagogue were fastened on him. 21 He began by saying to them, "Today this scripture is fulfilled in your hearing."

In this declaration, Jesus set his compass to true north, and his clarity meant that everyone who heard him understood what he was really about.

It is so important to understand who you are and why you are going to do something, such as starting an enterprise. In challenging times, you can remind yourself and other team members why you first set out on the journey.

Example: Cadbury & Clarks

Businesses transform lives! That may sound pretentious but it is true. Giving people dignity and purpose transforms lives. Offering people jobs and the means to provide for their families transforms lives. The theology of work has too often been reduced to a hunting ground for people to bring to church and the means by which you can give money - God save us!

Working is something that God expected of Adam when he was created (Genesis 2:15). And in Colossians 3:23 we read: "Work willingly at whatever you do, as though you were working for the Lord rather than for people."

God sees work as essential and it gives purpose to our lives. Therefore, enterprises that grow and provide employment and meaningful employment can transform the lives of those who feel a loss of purpose if they are out of work. Your enterprise could make a world of difference.

Faith-inspired enterprises that put as much emphasis on purpose as profit were prevalent throughout the 19th century. Household names that considered the needs of their workers include confectioner Cadbury and shoemaker Clarks. As well as providing employment, these enterprises improved working and social conditions for their employees and the community.

Both had their true north set at improving the lives of their workers. They did not sacrifice their 'why' for profit, and not only paid fair wages, but provided affordable homes for employees who were used to slums and squalor. Indeed, these entrepreneurs put transformation at the centre rather than transaction. Financial gain was not their driver, so they did not treat their workforce as citizens without worth. They returned work as a result, and hard work at that. Together, the businesses' owners and workers transformed not only their lives, but the lives of future generations. That is a truly transformative way to do business that is far removed from something merely transactional.

Discussion

As a group, discuss the good that you can create through business.

Step 1: Write your manifesto for WHY you are going to start a business. To help, please find the Business Transformation Template at the end of this section.

Prayer

Father God, as we start our journey, let the Holy Spirit guide us and give us clarity so that we discover our real motivation. Let our hearts be pure in what we want to achieve and let us not be driven purely by monetary gain nor self-importance. Give us a servant heart so that we understand that through our enterprise we are here to serve those who will work with and for us. In Jesus name we pray, Amen

Businesses transform lives!
Giving people dignity and purpose
transforms lives. Offering people jobs
and the means to provide for their
families transforms lives.

Business Transformation Template

Why are you starting a business?

For whom will your business create opportunities?

What value is it adding to society?

How many sustainable jobs do you hope it might create?

How much economic growth do think it might add to the nations economy?

Session 2

Innovation not Invention

Introduction

If you enjoy drinking wine, you may well have tried a wine club. While heading out to a vineyard in mainland Europe might be your preference, finding the time and money to do so might be difficult.

So instead, you may choose one of the many wine clubs to bring vineyards to your doorstep and to your glass. Prepare yourself for the delivery of the rather bland brown box with tasting notes thrown on top. I've even received tasting samples of wine in plastic bottles and taster bottles than belong in the chemistry lab rather than on the dining table. On occasion, there is a video call to join where, if you are not careful, you'll be hit with a PowerPoint presentation to help educate you about the facts around the wine.

In conversation with a friend about our love for wine, we felt we could innovate and create a "woah" experience for people. We believed that having beautifully packaged, high-quality presentation boxes with a professionally designed booklet rather than simple notes would make our offer stand out.

And instead of an online tasting event with snooze-inducing PowerPoints, we decided to create an immersive experience. A 'chat show' style online event with the guest sommelier who tastes the wine as you enjoy it at home, with the opportunity to ask questions would, we thought, make for a much better experience.

As a result of our conversation, we launched a new enterprise, called Rebottling.

Now, I don't want to sound like this is free advertising! I only share this with you to show that it really is possible to take something already in existence, innovate it and create a new product.

We're not claiming to have invented wine-tasting experiences but we have taken what was available and innovated it. The end result is a new product.

Changing a product or service by 10% is effectively creating something new. And it proves that you don't have to be a mad inventor to be an entrepreneur.

Be an innovator

Edison didn't invent the lightbulb, but innovated something that already existed! Although his bulb was revolutionary, it was an innovation, not an invention.

Nobel Prize-winning biochemist Dr Albert Szent-Györgyi said, "Innovation is seeing what everybody has seen and thinking what nobody has thought."

Have you seen a product or service you think could be altered or improved to produce a better end product? The technology company Apple highlights this nicely.

The personal computer was already in existence in 1976 when Apple founder and designer Steve Wozniak began innovating it. As well as being expensive, PCs were quite technical and out of the reach of most people.

As a result of Wozniak and his team's innovations, Apple created computers that were easy to use for a wider audience. They didn't invent the computer, but they innovated it so that it essentially became a new product.

Do you use products or services that you think you could improve through innovation? Remember, just 10% difference is enough to launch something new.

Reading: The great entrepreneur

From the very first book of the Bible, we see God is an entrepreneur. If you had to define an entrepreneur, you could say 'someone who takes a risk to create something for the good of others'.

In **Genesis 1: 1-31**, we see God acting to make something out of nothing, he is the 'great entrepreneur'.

1 In the beginning God created the heavens and the earth. 2 Now the earth was formless and empty, darkness was over the surface of the deep, and the Spirit of God was hovering over the waters.

3 And God said, "Let there be light," and there was light. 4 God saw that the light was good, and he separated the light from the darkness. 5 God called the light "day," and the darkness he called "night." And there was evening, and there was morning—the first day.

6 And God said, "Let there be a vault between the waters to separate water from water." 7 So God made the vault and separated the water under the vault from the water above it. And it was so. 8 God called the vault "sky." And there was evening, and there was morning—the second day.

9 And God said, "Let the water under the sky be gathered to one place, and let dry ground appear." And it was so. 10 God called the dry ground "land," and the gathered waters he called "seas." And God saw that it was good.

11 Then God said, "Let the land produce vegetation: seed-bearing plants and trees on the land that bear fruit with seed in it, according to their various kinds." And it was so. 12 The land produced vegetation: plants bearing seed according to their kinds and trees bearing fruit with seed in it according to their kinds. And God saw that it was good. 13 And there was evening, and there was morning—the third day.

14 And God said, "Let there be lights in the vault of the sky to separate the day from the night, and let them serve as signs to mark sacred times, and days and years, 15 and let them be lights in the vault of the sky to give light on the earth." And it was so. 16 God made two great lights—the greater light to govern the day and the lesser light to govern the night. He also made the stars. 17 God set them in the vault of the sky to give light on the earth, 18 to govern the day and the night, and to separate light from darkness. And God saw that it was good. 19 And there was evening, and there was morning—the fourth day.

20 And God said, "Let the water teem with living creatures, and let birds fly above the earth across the vault of the sky." 21 So God created the great creatures of the sea and every living thing with which the water teems and that moves about in it, according to their kinds, and every winged bird according to its kind. And God saw that it was good. *22* God blessed them and said, "Be fruitful and increase in number and fill the water in the seas, and let the birds increase on the earth." *23* And there was evening, and there was morning—the fifth day.

24 And God said, "Let the land produce living creatures according to their kinds: the livestock, the creatures that move along the ground, and the wild animals, each according to its kind." And it was so. *25* God made the wild animals according to their kinds, the livestock according to their kinds, and all the creatures that move along the ground according to their kinds. And God saw that it was good.

26 Then God said, "Let us make mankind in our image, in our likeness, so that they may rule over the fish in the sea and the birds in the sky, over the livestock and all the wild animals, and over all the creatures that move along the ground."

27 So God created mankind in his own image,
    in the image of God he created them;
    male and female he created them.

28 God blessed them and said to them, "Be fruitful and increase in number; fill the earth and subdue it. Rule over the fish in the sea and the birds in the sky and over every living creature that moves on the ground."

29 Then God said, "I give you every seed-bearing plant on the face of the whole earth and every tree that has fruit with seed in it. They will be yours for food. *30* And to all the beasts of the earth and all the birds in the *sky and all the creatures that move along the ground —everything that has the breath of life in it—I give every green plant for food." And it was so.*

31 God saw all that he had made, and it was very good. And there was evening, and there was morning—the sixth day.

For three days, God created the form and then spent three days creating content. As he created us to be in the image and likeness of the great entrepreneur, we also have the spirit of enterprise within us. As you re-read verse 28 it is explicit that God gives us the mandate and purpose to be fruitful, increase and rule. He expects us to be productive and multiply.

And being image-bearers of God, we can exercise the spirit of enterprise. We are made to generate ideas, create and innovate, it is who he has made us to be.

Example: Tesla

We have seen that many items used daily are not necessarily the direct result of the original inventor. Innovators turn something that merely exists into something that truly engages.

The car industry is awash with examples of innovation, none more so than Tesla! By taking the idea of electric cars and innovating them, Elon Musk has created one of the world's most sought after car brands.

What his company produces isn't inventive, as cars have existed since the early 19th century. The inventor of the petrol car we know today first came off production lines in 1887 thanks to Karl Benz.

Electric cars are not new, either. Electric vehicles pre-date those powered by petroleum, in fact, and were seen as an alternative to steam-powered vehicles years before!

Frustrated with electric vehicles from the big brands – which were generally quirky looking and generally ugly – Musk decided to innovate.

Taking ideas already in existence, he added some fun. From automatic steering to fun sound items within the car, Tesla brought together an element of motoring that would appeal to a tech-savvy generation.

As well as fun items, Tesla packaged its first cars as luxury saloons that looked unique but not ugly, proving electric could be mainstream!

Discussion

What things in the world around are frustrating that you could imagine being improved?

Step 2: What is your idea for improving an existing product/service? At the end of this session, you will find a Business Innovation Template to help you capture your ideas.

Prayer

Father in heaven, as we embark on a new journey, we ask that the Holy Spirit speaks to us. Give us the vision to take and innovate products and services that glorify your name. Help us understand the needs of others and how our ideas may make their lives better. In Jesus's name we ask this, Amen

If you had to define an entrepreneur, you could say 'someone who takes a risk to create something for the good of others'.

Business Innovation Template

Brainstorm what 10 things frustrate you?

What ideas do you have for solutions to these frustrations?

Which of these ideas do you thing are the best, either because of your passion or their feasibility?

You have to be passionate enough about a venture to make it succeed. But you must ensure that there is a felt need or it will fail to lift off.

Session 3
Felt need not Fanciful Passion

Introduction

After being made redundant, a friend resolved that the time was right to consider a career change. As someone who loved cooking, he looked at a new venture in food.

With so much competition at lunchtime, he thought he would try something different. He wanted to offer a healthier option to sandwiches, wraps and pastries.

Many people commented on his cooking, particularly his tasty soups and sauces. With this in mind, he decided to look at developing a new kind of lunchtime takeaway: soup! He even surmised that in the summer gazpacho and other groundbreaking cold soup creations would make enough profit to keep the business running in warm weather.

Strangely enough, he didn't think about how many people had a felt need for soup. In a large city, there may be a diverse enough audience. But in a small town, a takeaway bowl of soup was unlikely to be a daily wish list item!

Thankfully, my friend didn't just launch into the business. Instead, he carried out a bit of market research and discovered that it probably wouldn't work. His idea was a fanciful passion, and he realised that soup wouldn't draw enough customers.

Later, a new opportunity came his way, and he developed a different business.

Reading: Daily distribution of food

The lesson he learned was, that while his passion resulted in a tasty soup, others didn't share his enthusiasm. And it is a lesson we should all learn: check that your idea for enterprise is more than just your passion.

Of course, you have to be passionate enough about a venture to make it succeed. But you must ensure that there is a felt need or it will fail to lift off.

We can see a genuine felt need when reading from the book of Acts. In the first six verses of chapter six, there was a felt need in the community. We read that people were being overlooked in the daily distribution of food.

Acts 6: 1-6

6   *In those days when the number of disciples was increasing, the Hellenistic Jews[a] among them complained against the Hebraic Jews because their widows were being overlooked in the daily distribution of food. 2 So the 12 gathered all the disciples together and said, "It would not be right for us to neglect the ministry of the word of God in order to wait on tables. 3 Brothers and sisters, choose seven men from among you who are known to be full of the Spirit and wisdom. We will turn this responsibility over to them 4 and will give our attention to prayer and the ministry of the word."*

5 This proposal pleased the whole group. They chose Stephen, a man full of faith and of the Holy Spirit; also Philip, Procorus, Nicanor, Timon, Parmenas, and Nicolas from Antioch, a convert to Judaism. 6 They presented these men to the apostles, who prayed and laid their hands on them.

The result of the felt need was that an enterprise was launched by the 12 leaders. Seven men were appointed, with the responsibility of leading daily distribution of food.

What this shows us is that if we genuinely look and listen to our target markets and customer communities we will pretty soon discover their genuine felt needs.

Example: Testcard

History is littered with examples where fanciful passion leads to ventures failing. Pepsi decided to launch Pepsi Crystal in the 1990s, a cola-tasting clear drink. The company spent around $500 million in development but because there was no felt need it failed. The venture was no more than a fanciful passion!

Identify a felt need, however, and you are more likely to create an enterprise that offers a solution!

A couple of guys, one a doctor, were chatting one day at the school gates while they waited to collect their children. They talked about how people dislike the idea of going to a doctor. When it comes to some people, they have to be in dire straits before seeking medical help.

From this discussion, the entrepreneurial pair realised that they had identified a need. The men also realised some people are unable to access a doctors surgery.

With this in mind, they launched a business called TestCard in 2017. The company's at-home UTI testing kit turns a smartphone camera into a clinical-grade scanner.

It provides immediate results which you can share with a GP or other healthcare professional. There's no waiting, no doctor's visits, no laboratory and no need for healthcare experts to translate your results.

This example shows how identifying a felt need creates a worthy enterprise – and one recognised by many industry leaders who have endowed it with many awards. It now employs around 30 people, and in 2020, the company secured £4.5 million of funding. This cash injection will help the business develop new products.

This innovation, employment and improvement in personal health was all down to two people recognising a felt need. While it may have been a passion, the felt need had to come first or else there would have been no enterprise.

Discussion

Of your ideas which do you think meet genuine felt needs and for whom?

Step 3: What is the genuine felt need and problem that your business will solve for people? How will it make their lives better? Our Genuine Felt Need Template at the end of this session will help.

Prayer

Father, we ask that you will speak into our lives to help us find a need in our community. Help us to be led by your Holy Spirit and not our own selfish desires and passions. Open our eyes and hearts to the felt needs you would want us to meet. We ask this in Jesus's name. Amen

Business Marketing Template

Pain - what is the genuine felt need?

Product - what is the solution?

Place - where are you going to sell the product?

Price - how much are you pricing it at?

Promotion - how are you going to make it known?

Physical evidence - what environment do you need for the product?

People - what customer facing team do you need?

Planning is worthwhile and helps you consider your steps. But planning can also get in the way of progress if you're not careful.

Session 4 :
Launch and Learn not Plan and Perfect

Introduction

Fail to plan, and you will plan to fail! You have probably heard that saying before. It is often quoted by business advisers, especially in the early days of setting up an enterprise.

Planning is worthwhile and helps you consider your steps, focus your resources and spot possible pitfalls in advance. But planning can also get in the way of progress if you're not careful.

I have met many people who excitedly share their plans – and years later they're still perfecting it. Don't let planning turn to procrastination!

At some point, you have to take a step of faith; you have to launch and then learn as you go or else you'll never start! Don't leave that too late.

Planning to launch an enterprise is often associated with large tomes of projections, theories and expectations. Those kinds of business plans are needed when you go for institutional funding, but not at the start-up stage where plans are not so complex.

The nth degree

I remember attending a conference where Simon Woodroffe, the founder of Yo Sushi, was the guest speaker. With such a large business, you would expect his original plan was in-depth. Surprisingly, he wrote it on a cigarette packet!

He scribbled down his ideas and the rest, as they say, is history. After writing the initial plan, he launched and learned as he went. His story shows that he did not allow planning to take over his time in preparation.

Of course, at some point, Woodroffe needed to find funding, and an in-depth plan was necessary. What I took away from his discussion, however, was that when setting out, you don't need to plan to the nth degree!

Reading: Planning action

In these two books of the Bible, we see that planning is important, but that faith without action is dead!

First of all, we turn to **Luke 14, 28-31**

> 28 *"Suppose one of you wants to build a tower. Won't you first sit down and estimate the cost to see if you have enough money to complete it?* 29 *For if you lay the foundation and are not able to finish it, everyone who sees it will ridicule you,* 30 *saying, 'This person began to build and wasn't able to finish.'*
>
> 31 *"Or suppose a king is about to go to war against another king. Won't he first sit down and consider whether he is able with 10,000 men to oppose the one coming against him with 20,000?*

And then turn to **James 2: 14-18.**

> *14 What good is it, my brothers and sisters, if someone claims to have faith but has no deeds? Can such faith save them? 15 Suppose a brother or a sister is without clothes and daily food. 16 If one of you says to them, "Go in peace; keep warm and well fed," but does nothing about their physical needs, what good is it? 17 In the same way, faith by itself, if it is not accompanied by action, is dead.*
>
> *18 But someone will say, "You have faith; I have deeds." Show me your faith without deeds, and I will show you my faith by my deeds.*

What we learn here is that if we truly believe in our God-given idea we will make a plan and act upon it. God cannot bless your enterprise if it's no more than a plan. So take that step of faith and launch — then learn as you go.

Example: The Spirit of Enterprise

The Spirit of Enterprise initiative sums up what it means to launch and learn perfectly. Originally, the call for faith-inspired people to launch enterprises was the topic of The Times article I wrote and which you've already seen in the introduction to this book.

But the feedback that I received was clear: many people really loved the idea of transformational business and wanted to do something about it. Within 24 hours of the article appearing, I was chatting to my team at Cinnamon Network International about what the initiative could achieve.

Within the week of the article's appearance, we had assembled a steering group made up of some amazing people. We had also launched a website and social media and a news release was ready to go. Yes, there was a plan behind the start of The Spirit of Enterprise, but it was necessary to strike while the iron was hot!

Effectively, we got the plane in the air and started to build it. Entrepreneur Richard Branson started Virgin Airlines when an American Airlines flight he was due to board was cancelled.

He was so livid, that he asked his fellow frustrated passengers whether they would join him if he chartered an airplane. Marching to the back of the airport, he hired a plane and handed over his credit card.

Using a blackboard that he borrowed, he wrote, 'Virgin Airlines – one way $39.' After filling the plane he noticed an opportunity and literally launched the plane and built the business as he flew!

One of Branson's must famous quotes is: "If somebody offers you an amazing opportunity but you are not sure you can do it, say yes – then learn how to do it later!"

You can't plan forever, so get out, set up your enterprise and learn as you go.

Discussion

What are the benefits of launching and learning as you go?

Step 4: Write a one page business plan. Check out the template at the end of this session!

Prayer

Father in Heaven, help us honour your name by trusting you when we step out in faith. Give us peace in our hearts when we answer your call. Help us as we take our enterprise from idea to launch so that it reaches out and gives hope to others. This we ask in Jesus's name. Amen

You can't plan forever, so get out, set up your enterprise and learn as you go.

Business Plan Template

Genuine Felt Need:
What is the problem that you are going to solve and how?

Target Market:
Who are your customers/clients?

Innovation:
What product/service are you improving and how?

Industry Analysis:
What is your competition and what are your differentiating success factors?

Financial Summary:
What is your business model and the budget for the first 12 months?

Business Description:
What is you company going to do?

Implementation Timeline:
What are the headlines of what you are going to do over the short, medium and long-term?

Action Plan:
What are your MINS? (Most important Next Steps)?

Collaboration is the best way to build a successful enterprise because you cannot be an expert in everything.

Session 5 :
Soulmates not Solo

Introduction

Many people start an enterprise on their own – but that option means you may miss out on growing it effectively. While entrepreneurs set up their venture alone in the very earliest days, it doesn't take long to introduce others to the business.

The most successful entrepreneurs work with others because they recognise the need for teamwork. Collaboration is the best way to build a successful enterprise because you cannot be an expert in everything.

I have seen some business owners stretch themselves too far. They thought that as well as developing a product or service, they should also be the marketer, salesperson and finance department. You cannot spread yourself so thinly. In fact, you could argue that such an outlook is not entrepreneurial at all!

Aspen Institute's Entrepreneurship Strategy Group says collaboration is part of the entrepreneurial mindset. It outlines this mindset as a 'critical mix of success-oriented attitudes of initiative, intelligent risk-taking, collaboration and opportunity recognition'.

Building a team is essential in any business or enterprise. I remember speaking to a director of an accountancy firm who said his success was down to strategy when making appointments. Whenever he interviewed for positions within the business, he would make sure the person being appointed was better at the job than him. This, he concluded, meant he could focus on other aspects of the business because he knew the employee was doing a great job.

Don't live for yourself

The saying, 'no man is an island' expresses the idea that humans do badly when isolated. Indeed, the Bible confirms this! Romans 14:7 says, "For none of us lives for ourselves alone, and none of us dies for ourselves alone."

God did not create us to be alone; it is why he created Eve so that Adam would not be alone. In enterprise, this is not simply because we need the company of others, but we also work better as a team.

We have all been blessed with different gifts. While you may be a fantastic strategist, someone else within the enterprise could be much better at sales. There is no point having a team of people who have strengths in the same area.

Building teams is also important. Let's consider the football pitch. When building a team to play on the field, you don't choose 11 strikers! They may be able to score goals, but they won't be proficient at stopping attacks from the opposition.

Big businesses are run by boards of directors for a reason. Each director has a unique skill, and through collaboration they can see the wider picture of how a business is operating. Doing that solo would definitely lead to oversights and problems; no one can do more than one task at a time.

So while you are planning your enterprise, make sure you recruit others to help you. In the first instance, they may be volunteers or freelance contractors who have the experience to help you. But once the enterprise grows, there will be an opportunity to increase your team.

Reading: We are like a human body

Paul describes the Church as a body. Without all the different parts working together, the body is incomplete and does not function. This is also the case with enterprises: if all team members are good at the same thing, the venture will not work as well as it should.

1 Corinthians 12: 12-26

12 Just as a body, though one, has many parts, but all its many parts form one body, so it is with Christ. 13 For we were all baptised by one Spirit so as to form one body—whether Jews or Gentiles, slave or free—and we were all given the one Spirit to drink. 14 Even so the body is not made up of one part but of many.

15 Now if the foot should say, "Because I am not a hand, I do not belong to the body," it would not for that reason stop being part of the body. 16 And if the ear should say, "Because I am not an eye, I do not belong to the body," it would not for that reason stop being part of the body. 17 If the whole body were an eye, where would the sense of hearing be? If the whole body were an ear, where would the sense of smell be? 18 But in fact God has placed the parts in the body, every one of them, just as he wanted them to be. 19 If they were all one part, where would the body be? 20 As it is, there are many parts, but one body.

21 The eye cannot say to the hand, "I don't need you!" And the head cannot say to the feet, "I don't need you!" 22 On the contrary, those parts of the body that seem to be weaker are indispensable, 23 and the parts that we think are less honourable we treat with special honour. And the parts that are unpresentable are treated with special modesty, 24 while our presentable parts need no special treatment. But God has put the body together, giving greater honour to the parts that lacked it, 25 so that there should be no division in the body, but that its parts should have equal concern for each other. 26 If one part suffers, every part suffers with it; if one part is honoured, every part rejoices with it.

The reading clearly demonstrates that in order to be whole and complete, we need one another. God created us to function in interdependent relationships; if our business is to be successful we must do it with others by building a team.

Example: Apple

Steve Wozniak is a name you might not instantly recognise, although we have mentioned him earlier in this book. He was the technical genius behind Apple when it was founded in the 1970s. One of the reasons you may not recognise his name is because, like many inventive people, he was a quiet person who shunned the limelight.

Had Wozniak decided to work solo, Apple would not be the business it is today. Wozniak founded the business with Steve Jobs, a remarkable sales person who also had vision and understood strategy. A charismatic person, Jobs brought not only sales, but also awareness of the brand.

Using their different skills, they created a business and a dynamic team that helped Apple become the first company to be worth $1 trillion.

Discussion

What different aspects of enterprise will your team need to cover?

Step 5: Map out the capabilities and rôles you need to start your business. Then begin recruiting people whether as volunteers, freelance contractors or suppliers. The Business Team Template on the last page of this session will help.

Prayer

Father, you created us to be like a body where we work together. Help us to see the opportunity to bring the right people to the enterprise to make it flourish. We also ask that you will allow us to understand our limitations and allow others to use the skills you have given them. Amen

God created us to function in interdependent relationships; if our business is to be successful we must do it with others by building a team.

Business Team Template

Requirements/Functions/Capabilities	Provider
Partner	
Company Directors	
Coach	
Investor/s	
Accountant	
Bank	
Lawyer	
Marketing	
Operations	
Others	

Owning a smaller share in a large enterprise is better than owning all the shares in a small one.

Session 6 :
Size not Share

Introduction

Owning a micro business is undoubtedly a great achievement. But micro businesses are, by their very nature, restricted. With fewer people involved and less cash in the business than a large one, investment is limited and their growth is slower.

That is why owning a small share in a large business can give better returns than a complete or large share in a small one. Size matters more than share in such cases.

Enterprises that are hungry for growth will often sell small numbers of shares in their business to fund their expansion. This is called selling equity in the business and became a fairly common phrase thanks to TV show Dragon's Den.

Raising equity

I'll admit I no longer watch the programme as keenly as I used to. But Dragon's Den has demonstrated how many enterprises raise capital to drive their business growth forward: they sell equity in their business.

If you haven't seen the show, wealthy entrepreneurs and investors, known as 'Dragons', listen to a pitch from a business director or directors. The owners of the company hope that one or more 'Dragons' like what they hear and offer money for a share of the business. The cash will then be used to fund the first or next stage of business growth.

Now I know you may be thinking that you don't know anyone with the available sums of a multi-millionaire 'Dragon'. Selling equity, however, doesn't mean finding one or two wealthy funders — you can split this between more people who buy a smaller share of your enterprise.

Owning a smaller share in a large enterprise is better than owning all the shares in a small one. The investor takes on a lower risk because they are sharing the risk with more people.

How to find funders

Now, you may recognise the idea behind selling shares as the way that large companies raise capital on a stock market. But you do not need to be a FTSE100 firm to access this type of fund raising.

Crowdfunding is one of the ways that many companies sell equity. It is becoming increasingly popular and in 2020, UK businesses raised £103 million from crowdfunding.

This is split into different types of opportunities: seed, venture, growth and established. Seed funding is used by new businesses that have yet to be established and are looking for funding to start.

Venture, growth and established crowdfunding is for businesses already in existence. As the name for each explains, you choose the type depending on the plans you have and the stage you're at.

The alternatives

Selling equity in your enterprise is a useful way of funding your enterprise, whether to get it off the ground or for specific projects or plans.

Some people may offer other ways of funding such proposals, for example using savings, asking family or friends for a 'soft loan' or visiting a bank.

Using savings means you take on all the risk: if the enterprise fails to see good returns, you may lose all your money. If the enterprise is successful, organic growth might also fund future developments, but this tends to be slow.

The alternative is to secure a loan. Many business owners might choose a friend or family member for a 'soft loan'. But this could put pressure on relationships if the enterprise isn't as successful as planned.

Bank loans are also an option, but there are many hoops to jump through and all the paperwork can make it a slow process. So selling equity is a smart way of attracting funding that can help your enterprise grow.

What you need to do

To sell shares in your enterprise you must do some groundwork. People will not simply hand over cash unless they understand why you need it. You will need to show that you have done your homework and cover a number of items including:

- Investment deal details (such as valuation of your enterprise)

- Business plans (including financial forecasts and strategy)
- Market analysis (the size and growth of the market)
- Team (executive team and board director profiles)

All of this information needs bringing together into a pitch deck document. This contains all the details a potential investor needs to know to help them decide if your opportunity is right for them.

Reading: Investing based on ability

Investing in others is something God encourages. He has created an ecosystem of innovators and investors who need one another in order be good managers of what he entrusted them with. We see this in Matthew 25: 14-30.

Matthew 25:14-30

14 "Again, it will be like a man going on a journey, who called his servants and entrusted his wealth to them. 15 To one he gave five bags of gold, to another two bags, and to another one bag, each according to his ability. Then he went on his journey. 16 The man who had received five bags of gold went at once and put his money to and gained five bags more. 17 So also, the one with two bags of gold gained two more. 18 But the man who had received one bag went off, dug a hole in the ground and hid his master's money.

19 "After a long time the master of those servants returned and settled accounts with them. 20 The man who had received five bags of gold brought the other five. 'Master,' he said, 'you entrusted me with five bags of gold. See, I have gained five more.'

21 "His master replied, 'Well done, good and faithful servant! You have been faithful with a few things; I will put you in charge of many things. Come and share your master's happiness!'

22 "The man with two bags of gold also came. 'Master,' he said, 'you entrusted me with two bags of gold; see, I have gained two more.'

23 "His master replied, 'Well done, good and faithful servant! You have been faithful with a few things; I will put you in charge of many things. Come and share your master's happiness!'

24 "Then the man who had received one bag of gold came. 'Master,' he said, 'I knew that you are a hard man, harvesting where you have not sown and gathering where you have not scattered seed. 25 So I was afraid and went out and hid your gold in the ground. See, here is what belongs to you.'

26 "His master replied, 'You wicked, lazy servant! So you knew that I harvest where I have not sown and gather where I have not scattered seed? 27 Well then, you should have put my money on deposit with the bankers, so that when I returned I would have received it back with interest.

28 "'So take the bag of gold from him and give it to the one who has ten bags. 29 For whoever has will be given more, and they will have an abundance. Whoever does not have, even what they have will be taken from them. 30 And throw that worthless servant outside, into the darkness, where there will be weeping and gnashing of teeth.'

What Jesus highlights in these verses is that people are entrusted with resources according to their ability to use them well. Those people who are good managers of the resources entrusted to them will be entrusted with more.

God clearly does not want us to hide away what has been entrusted to us, but to share it.

Example: BrewDog

When the owners of brewing company BrewDog decided they wanted to raise funds to invest in expanding its range, they chose to ignore traditional routes.

Knowing that their customers were also great brand ambassadors, they turned to them to encourage them to help fund the company's growth.

They decided to ignore crowdfunding and set up their own 'Equity for Punks' scheme. Owning a share of the business means their customers not only have a say in the company, they also receive special gifts, such as glasses and brewery visits.

It has been such a success that there have been other equity sales, including the most recent plan to help them install solar power in their breweries.

Discussion

Who would believe in your proposition and put cash in to start your business?

Step 6: Write a list of family, friends and connections who are prospective investors. Start conversations with people. Prepare a pitch deck, a template is included at the end of the session.

Prayer

Heavenly Father, help lead us to supportive people who can help our enterprise grow and change lives. We pray for connections to those who understand our aims and ambitions. Help us be good managers of the finances we receive so that we can use them to improve the lives of others through this venture. We ask it in the name of Jesus. Amen

Pitch Deck Template

Title page with
your logo

Pitch Deck Template

Product/Service Description & Picture

Pitch Deck Template

Size and Growth of the Market

Pitch Deck Template

Competitor Analysis & Differentiation

Pitch Deck Template

Team (Bios & Pics)

Pitch Deck Template

Contact details

It is only natural when setting up a business or enterprise that you will have moments where you feel inadequate.

Session 7
Leadership not Limitations

Introduction

If I asked you to name an inspirational leader, who would spring to mind? And what if I asked about the traits that made that person a leader? I do not doubt that you would offer a long list of their strengths.

We are guilty of looking upon leaders as being infallible because we only ever see their positive aspects. As a result of this misconception, you can conclude that your flaws mean you are not the right person to lead.

Ask any leader about themselves, and I am sure they would admit to having limitations, however. What makes them stand out is they do not focus on their shortcomings.

If entrepreneurs spent time concentrating on their flaws, enterprises would never get off the ground. So if you are considering launching an enterprise but have a long list of limitations, let me encourage you to ignore them.

It is only natural when setting up a business or enterprise that you will have moments where you feel inadequate. And there will be times when you believe you could do better or you make a mistake. But this is all part of the learning curve!

Wear failure like a badge

Sundar Pichai, the CEO of Google and its parent company Alphabet, says leaders should wear 'failure like a badge'. And he tells people not to be disheartened by shortcomings; but to learn from them and allow them to transform how you lead.

The Spirit of Enterprise needs people who will take a leap of faith, which you cannot do if paralysed by your limitations.

Leaders who focus on their limitations are not new, of course. Moses was quite clear: during his encounter with God at the burning bush he insisted that his limitations made him a terrible choice as a leader.

But once he agreed to step up to the plate, he became a courageous and transformational leader.

Reading: Moses leadership and limitations

Exodus 4:1-17

> Moses answered, "What if they do not believe me or listen to me and say, 'The Lord did not appear to you'?"
>
> 2 Then the Lord said to him, "What is that in your hand?"
>
> A staff," he replied.
>
> 3 The Lord said, "Throw it on the ground."
>
> Moses threw it on the ground and it became a snake, and he ran from it. 4 Then the Lord said to him, "Reach

out your hand and take it by the tail." So Moses reached out and took hold of the snake and it turned back into a staff in his hand.

5 "This," said the Lord, "is so that they may believe that the Lord, the God of their fathers—the God of Abraham, the God of Isaac and the God of Jacob— has appeared to you."

6 Then the Lord said, "Put your hand inside your cloak." So Moses put his hand into his cloak, and when he took it out, the skin was leprous[a]—it had become as white as snow.

7 "Now put it back into your cloak," he said. So Moses put his hand back into his cloak, and when he took it out, it was restored, like the rest of his flesh.

8 Then the Lord said, "If they do not believe you or pay attention to the first sign, they may believe the second.

9 But if they do not believe these two signs or listen to you, take some water from the Nile and pour it on the dry ground. The water you take from the river will become blood on the ground."

10 Moses said to the Lord, "Pardon your servant, Lord. I have never been eloquent, neither in the past nor since you have spoken to your servant. I am slow of speech and tongue."

11 The Lord said to him, "Who gave human beings their mouths? Who makes them deaf or mute? Who gives them sight or makes them blind? Is it not I, the Lord? 12 Now go; I will help you speak and will teach you what to say."

13 But Moses said, "Pardon your servant, Lord. Please send someone else."

14 Then the Lord's anger burned against Moses and he said, "What about your brother, Aaron the Levite?

I know he can speak well. He is already on his way to meet you, and he will be glad to see you. 15 You shall speak to him and put words in his mouth; I will help both of you speak and will teach you what to do. 16 He will speak to the people for you, and it will be as if he were your mouth and as if you were God to him. 17 But take this staff in your hand so you can perform the signs with it."

Moses pointed out five self-limitations that he felt ruled him out of leadership: he was not good enough; he didn't have all the answers; people wouldn't believe him; he was a poor public speaker; and he wasn't qualified.

What he wasn't expecting was that God already had everything in place. He can use our skills and resources that appear ineffectual and use them to meet his needs. In verse 2, he had already put in Moses's hand the staff, and he has already put in your hand the gifts he can use.

Using self-limitations as an excuse can feel like authentic justification for failing to achieve. But in verses 10-12, God explains clearly that he has given Moses all he needs: a mouth and the ability to speak. He, like you, has the basics, so the only stumbling blocks are your own self-limitations.

And as we have already agreed, we are meant to be working with soulmates; not solo. In verses 13-17, God highlights the importance of teamwork. Having a number of people using their strengths together forms formidable partnerships. Look around at whom God might have brought into your life.

Prayer

Father, you have given me gifts of the spirit that I sometimes cannot see and do not use. Forgive me for the times that I have used excuses instead of stepping out and answering your call. Like Moses, Lord, I often focus too much on my self-limitations. But you have given me, like him, the ability to lead.

Help me find reasons to do your will rather than excuses that prevent me from taking the step into leadership.

Amen

Using self-limitations as an excuse can feel like authentic justification for failing to achieve.

Leadership Plan Template

Self-leadership: How are you transforming yourself?

Product/Service leadership: How are you developing the delivery of your product & service?

Organisational leadership: How are you growing your organisation?

Now is the time for you and me to ask God to reveal his gifting and call to us to create change. In an era of increasing despondency, we need to offer hope.

Conclusion

When my article appeared in The Times, I was excited to see what the response would be. I expected that some people would grasp the nettle, hear the call and start talking about the Spirit of Enterprise. I also expected a number of detractors, to be honest, who challenged the very thought of churches and Christians leading enterprise.

What happened was both exhilarating and humbling: suddenly, I received dozens of communications saying the article was the right message at the right time. None of the comments I received were negative!

Within one week, The Spirit of Enterprise launched with an experienced and thrilling steering group in what appears to be a real move of God. Even this very book has come together so incredibly quickly and efficiently, that it proves to me that God has made this call.

I hope that the sessions and templates provide the launchpad for your enterprises.

God has given us the gift of enterprise, he is the great entrepreneur and throughout Scripture we see enterprising people taking steps of faith to transform their communities.

Now is the time for you and me to ask God to reveal his gifting and call to us to create change. In an era of increasing despondency, we need to offer hope.

Faith needs action. We can all speak confidently of our faith to others but for those in real despair, actions speak louder than words. This is why it is important to provide the enterprises, the employment and the hope that provides more than just money.

While finances are essential, the Spirit of Enterprise offers true wealth: hope, dignity and relationships. From these we can all build enterprises that demonstrate God's love in action.

About Matt Bird

Matt Bird is a Global Speaker, Entrepreneur and Founder CEO of Cinnamon Network International helping churches transform communities.

He has spoken in 40 countries to more than a million people, authored more than a dozen books and is a regular broadcaster on radio, television and social media.

He is also the Founder CEO of Issachar Global helping people understand the times and how to live and lead, Relationology International helping leaders and their organisations build profitable relationships and Rebottling providing experiences of the greatest wines guided by the greatest sommeliers in the comfort of your home.

Matt lives in Wimbledon, England with his wife Esther and their three children.

Why not meet Matt online for a virtual coffee...

www.coffeewithmatt.com

About Cinnamon Network International

Cinnamon Network helps churches transform community.

- The **Cinnamon Transformation Pathway** supports churches to discern community needs and opportunities and replicate social enterprise projects with a track record for impact.

- The **Cinnamon Faith Action Audit** enables churches in a local government area to work together to measure their collective impact in order to catalyse their civic transformation journey.

- The **Cinnamon Spirit of Enterprise** resources churches to support people with ideas to start a businesses enterprise that creates social value, sustainable employment and economic growth.

Cinnamon Network International is developing resources and courses as well as networks in more than a dozen countries across four continents.

www.cinnamonnetwork.com

Resources

All the SoE Business Plan Templates as featured in this book can be downloaded as a multi-page A4 PDF by going to the following link:

www.thespiritofenterprise.net/templates

Other Books

Transformation

Transform

The Spirit of Enterprise

Replicate *(coming soon)*

www.mattbirdpublishing.com

Printed in Great Britain
by Amazon